PUPIL'S BOOK

My name is _____ .

Carol Read • Mark Ormerod

macmillan
education

Syllabus

	Key vocabulary	Key structures
How are you, Tiger?	hello, hi | play, speak, sing, count, listen, read, write | climb a tree, eat ice cream, play on a swing, ride a bike | numbers 1–20, colours | apple, ball, bike, children, ice cream | days of the week, classroom objects	How are you? I'm fine, thank you. | What's your name? How old are you? I'm (eight). Let's be friends. | How many (bikes)? Where's (number 16)? It's on the (skateboard). | Today is (Monday). Can I have a (pencil), please? Here you are. Thank you.
1 A Surprise	toilet, bedroom, bathroom, hall, living room, dining room, kitchen, garage | behind, in, next to, under | bed, fridge, clock, cooker, shower, sofa | flat, house, houseboat **Cross-curricular:** Social Science: Things in our home	Where's (Jay)? Is (he) (in) the (hall)? Yes, (he) is./ No, (he) isn't. | The (fridge) is in the (kitchen). Have you got a (clock) in your (bedroom)? Yes, I have./ No, I haven't. | I live in a (flat).
2 A New Pet	bird, hamster, turtle, kitten, rabbit, lizard, fish, puppy | leaves, seeds, meat, fish, grass, insects | guinea pig **Cross-curricular:** Natural Science: What pets eat	What has (she) got? Has (she) got a (lizard)? Yes, (she) has./No, (she) hasn't. (She) hasn't got a (rabbit). | My (brother) has got a (rabbit). (Rabbits) eat (grass).
3 Where's my coat?	shorts, shirt, coat, jumper, trousers, T-shirt, skirt, shoes and socks | spring, summer, autumn, winter, flower, tree | jeans, scarf **Cross-curricular:** Social Science: Seasons and nature	Is this your (coat)? I'm/You're wearing (my coat). | In (spring), you can see (flowers) on the tree. (My) favourite season is (winter). I like (spring). It's my favourite season. In this picture, it's (winter). I'm wearing (a hat).
4 Break Time	board game, hide and seek, football, basketball, cards, tag, hopscotch, computer game | classroom, gym, corridor, library, canteen, playground | leapfrog, rock, paper, scissors **Cross-curricular:** Social Science: School rules	I want to play (football). Do you want to play (cards)? | You can/ can't (play ball games) in the (classroom). | At break time, I play (leapfrog) in the (playground).
5 What's the matter?	toothache, headache, cough, cut, earache, cold, tummy ache, sore throat | drink water, wash, do exercise, eat well, play, sleep well | brush my teeth **Cross-curricular:** Natural Science: Keeping healthy	What's the matter? I'm feeling (ill). I've got (a headache). | Have you got (a cut)? Yes, I have./ No, I haven't. | I (do exercise) every day. Do you (sleep well) every day?
6 On Holiday	beach, water park, zoo, funfair, aquarium, park, ice rink, swimming pool | stop, stand on the pavement, look left, look right, listen, cross the road | cinema **Cross-curricular:** Social Science: Road safety	There's (an ice rink). Is there (an aquarium)? Yes, there is./No, there isn't. | Don't (stand in the road). | In my town, there's a (park).
Families	granny, grandad, mum, dad, brother, sister | piano, guitar, sing, dance | wash the car, set the table, do the shopping, wash the dishes	plural and singular nouns | I can (dance). I can't (play the piano). | I've got to (help Dad). I've got to (wash the dishes).
Tiger Tasks 1	**Learning outcomes:** **Mathematics:** read about and count family members using bar graphs **Music:** listen and identify different musical instruments	**Social Science:** write a letter about helping at home **Collaborative task:** make a poster and present it to your class
People, Places and Activities	hike, fish, cycle, park, mountains, river | months of the year, ordinal numbers 1st–31st | city, shops, tourists	You can (hike) in the (mountains). | When is your birthday? My birthday is on the (21st of May). | There are some (parks). There are lots of (mountains). There are many (shops).
Tiger Tasks 2	**Learning outcomes:** **Social Science:** read and think about activities we can do outdoors **Mathematics:** listen and understand a calendar	**Social Science:** write a fact file and learn about two places **Collaborative task:** make a collage and present it to your class
Festivals	**Halloween:** monster, spider, wizard, moon, skeleton	I've got a surprise for you. What is it? Look in the box. It's a (monster). Happy Halloween!
	Christmas: Father Christmas, Christmas card, Christmas stocking, Christmas cake, snowflake	Look! I've got a Christmas card. What's the picture? It's (Father Christmas). Happy Christmas!
	Carnival: king, pirate, cowboy, queen, clown	It's Carnival time. I'm wearing fancy dress. What am I? You're (a pirate).

	Vocabulary	Structures	Final Outcome
Focus on Andalusia **Topic 1: Places in Andalusia**	forest, beach, mountain, river, cave, shop, castle, square next to, behind, near, between, in front of go skiing, buy food, go swimming	The forest is next to the river. You / we can (go skiing) here. The weather is sunny and very hot. There's a castle. There are (fantastic) caves. Is there (a beach) in El Bosque? Are there (restaurants) in El Bosque? Yes, there is / are. No there isn't / aren't. There are lots of good restaurants.	**Vocabulary:** Identify different places and geographical features. **Reading (Postcard):** Read and understand a postcard. **Speaking:** Talk about a place. **Reading and writing (Text message):** Read and write a text message. **Project:** Create a postcard.
Focus on Andalusia **Topic 2: Food in Andalusia**	fried fish, meatballs, shrimp fritters, cold tomato soup, Spanish omelette, egg and chips, spinach and chickpeas, lentils months of the year horses, dresses, costumes prices	I / we eat ... People eat (Spanish omelette). You can see (lots of horses). When is the Feria in Seville? What can you see / eat? Cádiz has a big carnival in February. People celebrate the patios. What are we going to do / eat? How about ...? We can have ... I like ...	**Vocabulary:** Identify different types of Andalusian food. **Reading (Webpage):** Read a tourism webpage. **Speaking:** Talk about celebrations and food. **Reading and writing (Invitation):** Read and write a birthday party invitation. **Project:** Create a restaurant menu.

How are you, Tiger?

Lesson 1

1 Find and colour the names.

2 Listen, repeat and mime. 1:02

3 Listen, point and sing *Let's have fun in English*. 1:03

Key learning outcomes: review greetings; listen to, sing and act out a song
Language: *Hello. Hi. How are you? I'm fine, thank you. play, speak, sing, count, listen, read, write*

3

Lesson 2

4 Listen and write. 🔊 1:04 ✏️

5 Make the puppets (TB, p175). Act out the dialogue. ✂️ 💬

6 Listen, point and mime. Sing *Come to the park*. 🔊 1:05 🎵

Hi, I'm Sue. I'm nine.

I'm Jay. I'm seven.

I'm Li. I'm _____.

Key learning outcomes: act out a dialogue; listen to and sing a song
Language: *What's your name? How old are you? I'm (eight). Let's be friends.*
climb a tree, eat ice cream, play on a swing, ride a bike, numbers 1–9

4

Lesson 3

7 Listen and say *The number chant.*  1:06
Find and trace the numbers.

8 Find and count. Write the number. Listen and check. 1:07

a

20

b

c

d

Key learning outcome: identify and say numbers 10–20
Language: *How many (bikes)? Where's (number 16)? It's on the (skateboard).*
apple, ball, bike, children, ice cream, colours, numbers 10–20

5

Lesson 4

9 Listen, point and say *The days of the week chant.* 🔊 1:08 💬
Find and circle the classroom objects. ✏️

Today is _____ .

Monday
Tuesday
Wednesday
Thursday
Friday
Saturday
Sunday

Class Chat

10 Listen, number and repeat. Ask and answer. 🔊 1:09 ✏️ 💬

a Can I have a rubber, please?

1

b

c

d

Key learning outcomes: identify and say the days of the week; use classroom language
Language: *Today is (Monday). Can I have a (pencil), please? Here you are. Thank you.*
days of the week, classroom objects

A Surprise

Lesson 1 Vocabulary

1 Listen, look and repeat. 1:13

2 Listen, point and say *Tiger's word chant.* 1:14

3 Stick and say. Play *Can you remember?*

toilet

bedroom

bathroom

hall

living room

dining room

kitchen

garage

Key learning outcome: say and understand rooms vocabulary
Vocabulary: *toilet, bedroom, bathroom, hall, living room, dining room, kitchen, garage*

Lesson 2 Story

 4 **Listen to the story. Answer the questions.**
Play *Who says …?*
1:15

Storytime

1

Sue, Jay and Li are in the hall.

… 10, 11, 12, 13 …

2

I can hide in this cupboard.

I can hide next to this plant.

3

Can I play, Sue?

Yes, Tiger.

I can hide in this cupboard.

4

Where's Jay?
Is he in the hall?

Key learning outcome: listen to and understand a story
Story language: *Where's (Jay)? Is (he) (in) the (hall)? Yes, (he) is./No, (he) isn't. behind, in, next to, under*

Tiger Values

When you play games, do you let everyone play?

Lesson 3 Story activities

5 Listen and say the missing words.
1:16

6 Listen and tick (✔) the rooms Sue looks in.
1:17
Sing *Where's Li?* Look and write.

① ✔

hall

②

③

④

⑤

⑥

⑦

⑧

7 Listen, look and say who. Complete the sentences. 🔊 💬 ✏️
1:19

Tiger

Jay

Sue

① Tiger is in the _____*bathroom*_____ .

② Jay is in the _____ .

③ Sue is in the _____ .

Key learning outcome: use rooms vocabulary and story language
Language: *Where's (Jay)? Is (he) (in) the (hall)? Yes, (he) is./No, (he) isn't. behind, in, next to, under*

Lesson 4 Speaking

8 Listen, look and say. 1:20

Tiger Phonics

rubber
cupboard

9 Make the cut-out on page 99. Do a role play. ✂ 💬

Is Li in the kitchen?

No, she isn't.

Is Tiger under the pencil case?

Yes, he is.

Over To You

10 Play *Find Tiger*. 💬

Key learning outcome: practise pronunciation and do a role play
Language: *Is (Li) (in) the (kitchen)? Yes, (she) is./No, (she) isn't. behind, in, next to, under*
Phonics: *The cup and the rubber run under the cupboard.*

Things in our home

Lesson 5 Cross-curricular

11 Listen, point and say. Read and stick. 1:21

 **1**   **2**    **3**   **4**    **5**    **6**

bed					

12 Listen and repeat. Play *Observation*.   1:22

Ping and Pong

Key learning outcome: identify and talk about household objects
Vocabulary: *bed, fridge, clock, cooker, shower, sofa*

Lesson 6 Cross-curricular

13 Listen, match and repeat. 🔊 1:23 ✏️ 💬

14 Listen and point. Sing *The shower is in the bathroom.* 🔊 1:24 🎵
Mime and say. 💬

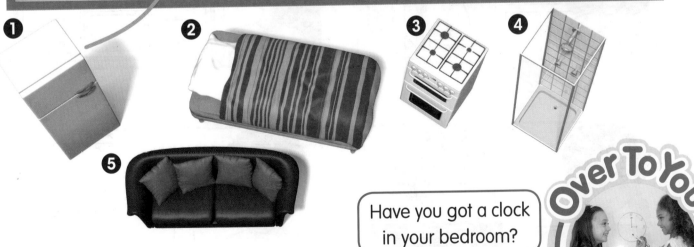

1 **2** **3** **4** **5**

Have you got a clock in your bedroom?

Over To You

15 Play *Draw and ask.* 💬

Key learning outcome: say what objects you have in your home
Language: *The (fridge) is in the (kitchen). Have you got a (clock) in your (bedroom)?*
Yes, I have./No, I haven't.

13

16 Listen, number and repeat. Complete the sentences.

1:25

She's in the ___bathroom___.

He's in the _____.

He's in the _____.

She's in the _____.

She's in the _____.

He's in the _____.

She's in the _____.

He's in the _____.

17 Look and write. Complete the sentences. ✏️

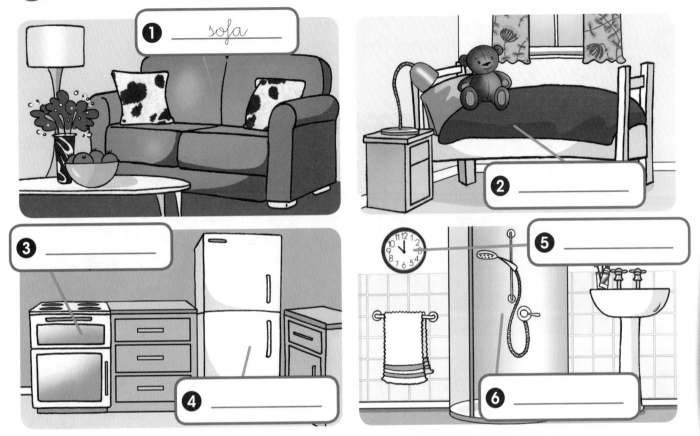

1 ___sofa___

2 _____

3 _____

4 _____

5 _____

6 _____

The _____ is in the living room.
The _____ is in the bedroom.

18 Listen, point and repeat. Ask and answer. 🔊 1:26 💬

Class Chat

Where's the teacher?

Learning to **LEARN**

➡️ Go to the Picture Dictionary on page 96.

1 **Listen and say a traditional rhyme:** *In a dark, dark house.*
Act it out. 🔊 1:27 🎵 📹

2 **Listen and number. Draw and write.** 🔊 1:28 ✏️ ✏️

Comparing Cultures

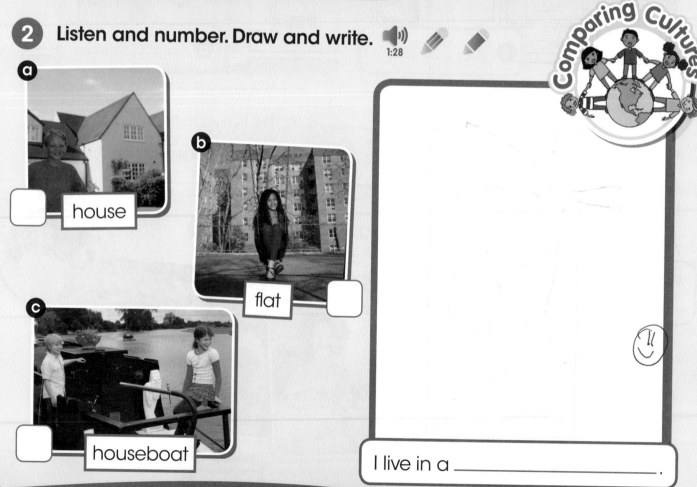

a [ ] house

b [ ] flat [ ]

c [ ] houseboat

I live in a _____.

Key learning outcome: listen to, say and act out a traditional rhyme
Language: *I live in a (flat).* house, flat, houseboat

2 A New Pet

Lesson 1 Vocabulary

1 Listen, look and repeat. 🔊 1:31 💬

2 Listen, point and say *Tiger's word chant*. 🔊 1:32 💬

3 Stick and say. Play *Can you remember?* 💬

1 bird

2 hamster

3 turtle

4 kitten

5 rabbit

6 lizard

7 fish

8 puppy

Key learning outcome: say and understand pets vocabulary
Vocabulary: *bird, hamster, turtle, kitten, rabbit, lizard, fish, puppy*

17

2

Lesson 2 Story

4 Listen to the story. Answer the questions.
Play *Who says …?*
1:33

Story time

1. Look! Li has got a new pet.

2. What has she got?

3. Has she got a hamster?

4. She hasn't got a lizard.

18

Key learning outcome: listen to and understand a story
Story language: *What has (she) got? Has (she) got a (lizard)? Yes, (she) has./No, (she) hasn't. (She) hasn't got a (rabbit).*

5

I think she's got a rock.

6

Help! Tiger has got my new pet.

7

It's a turtle.

His name's Tommy.

8

Look! Tommy has got a friend.

Tiger Values

If you've got a pet, do you look after it well?

Lesson 3 Story activities

5 Listen and say the missing words. 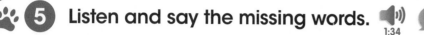 1:34

6 Listen and circle Li's pet. Sing *She's got a new pet.* 1:35
Look and write.

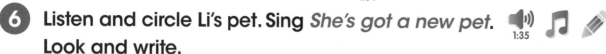

1 ___fish___ **2** _____ **3** _____ **4** _____

5 _____ **6** _____ **7** _____ **8** _____

7 Listen, look and say who. Complete the sentences. 1:37

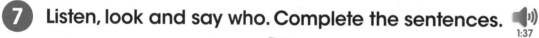

Tiger   Jay   Sue

1 Has Tiger got a ___kitten___? Yes, he has.

2 Has Jay got a _____? Yes, he has.

3 Has Sue got a _____? Yes, she has.

Key learning outcome: use pets vocabulary and story language
Language: *What has (she) got? Has (she) got a (lizard)? Yes, (she) has./No, (she) hasn't. (She) hasn't got a (rabbit).*

8 Listen, look and say.
1:38

rabbit
room

Tiger Phonics

Ricky

9 Make the cut-out on page 101. Do a role play.

Has Li got a rabbit?

No, she hasn't.

Bingo!

10 Play *Sentence bingo*.

Key learning outcome: practise pronunciation and do a role play
Language: *Has (Li) got a (rabbit)? Yes, (she) has./No, (she) hasn't.*
Phonics: *Ricky rabbit runs round and round the room.*

What pets eat

Lesson 5 Cross-curricular

11 Listen, point and say. Read and stick. 🔊 1:39

 ❶  ❷  ❸  ❹  ❺  ❻

| leaves | | | | | |

12 Listen and repeat. Play *Observation*. 🔊 1:40

Ping and Pong

❶ Rabbits don't eat meat, Pong.

❷ Parrots eat fruit and seeds.

❸

❹ Lizards eat leaves and insects.

❺

❻

Key learning outcome: identify and talk about what pets eat
Vocabulary: *leaves, seeds, meat, fish, grass, insects*

Lesson 6 Cross-curricular

13 Listen, colour and repeat. 🔊 1:41 ✏️ 💬

14 Listen and point. Sing *Different pets, different food.* 🔊 1:42 🎵

❶  ❷  ❸

❹  ❺

My brother has got a rabbit. Rabbits eat grass.

15 Talk about pets you know. 💬

Over To You

Key learning outcome: talk about pets you know and what they eat
Language: *My (brother) has got a (rabbit). (Rabbits) eat (grass).*

23

Lesson 7 Unit review

16 Listen, number and repeat. Complete the sentences.

1:43

a

He's got a ___*bird*___ .

b

She's got a _____ .

c

He's got a _____ .

d

1

She's got a _____ .

e

He's got a _____ .

f

She's got a _____ .

g

He's got a _____ .

h

She's got a _____ .

17 Look and write. Complete the sentences. ✏️

1

_____seeds_____

2

_____

3

_____

4

_____

5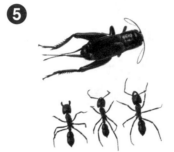

_____

6

_____

Dogs eat _____.

Lizards eat leaves and _____.

18 Listen, point and repeat. Ask and answer. 🔊 1:44 💬

Has everyone got a pen, a pencil and a book?

Class Chat

Learning to **LEARN**

→ Go to the Picture Dictionary on page 96.

1 **Listen and say a traditional rhyme:** *Two little dicky birds*.
Act it out. 1:45

Two little dicky birds …

… sitting on a wall.

PETER

PAUL

Comparing Cultures

2 **Listen and number. Draw and write.** 1:46

a
guinea pig

b
dog

c
rabbit

My _____ has got
a _____.

Key learning outcome: listen to, say and act out a traditional rhyme
Language: *My (friend) has got a (dog), guinea pig*

Tiger Review

1 Have you got any pets?

2 Listen to the story. Who is on the fridge? 1:47

❶ Where's Tiger?

He's in the living room.

❷ It's a hamster!

Don't open the door!

❸ It's under the sofa!

No. It's in the kitchen!

❹ It's on the fridge, next to the clock.

❺ Come here, little hamster!

My nose!

❻ Hello, Tiger!

Monkey and Mouse love your pets!

3 What pets have Sue and Jay got?

4 Look, listen and match. 🔊 1:48 ✏️

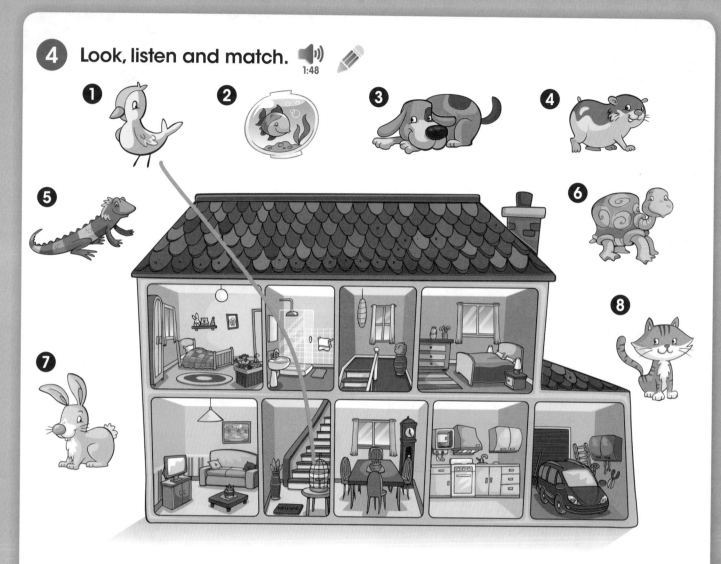

5 Look, ask and answer. 💬

Has he got a kitten?

No, he hasn't.

6 Listen and choose. 🔊 1:49
Sing your favourite song. 🎵

7 Think and colour. 💡 ✏️

Where's my coat?

Lesson 1 Vocabulary

1 Listen, look and repeat. 2:05

2 Listen, point and say *Tiger's word chant*. 2:06

3 Stick and say. Play *Can you remember?*

❶ shorts

❷ shirt

❸ coat

❹ jumper

❺ trousers

❻ T-shirt

❼ skirt

❽ shoes and socks

Lesson 2 Story

4 Listen to the story. Answer the questions.
Play *Who says ...?* 2:07

Key learning outcome: listen to and understand a story
Story language: *Is this your (coat)? I'm/You're wearing (my coat)*

Tiger Values

Do you always ask before you use other people's things?

3

Lesson 3 Story activities

5 Listen and say the missing words. 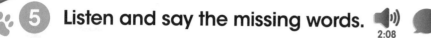 2:08

6 Listen and colour the clothes Tiger is wearing. 2:09

Sing *I'm wearing a coat.* Look and write.

1 ___coat___

2 _____

3 _____

4 _____

5 _____

6 _____

7 _____ and _____

8 _____

7 Listen, look and say who. Complete the sentences. 2:11

1 Look! I'm wearing a green ___skirt___.

Sue

2 Look! I'm wearing a red _____.

Jay

3 Look! I'm wearing blue _____ and orange _____.

Li

Key learning outcome: use clothes vocabulary and story language
Language: *I'm/You're wearing (my coat).*

Lesson 4 Speaking

8 Listen, look and say.
2:12

shirt
shorts

Tiger Phonics

9 Make the cut-out on page 103. Listen and fold.

I'm wearing shorts.

You're wearing a blue shirt.

Over To You

10 Play *What am I wearing?*

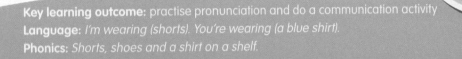

Key learning outcome: practise pronunciation and do a communication activity
Language: *I'm wearing (shorts). You're wearing (a blue shirt).*
Phonics: *Shorts, shoes and a shirt on a shelf.*

Seasons and nature

Lesson 5 Cross-curricular

11 Listen, point and say. Read and stick. 2:13

1 spring

2

3

4

5

6

12 Listen and repeat. Play *Observation*. 2:14

Ping and Pong

Key learning outcome: identify and talk about the seasons and nature
Vocabulary: *spring, summer, autumn, winter, flower, tree*

Lesson 6 Cross-curricular

13 Listen, number and repeat. 2:15

14 Listen and point. Sing *What's your favourite season?* 2:16
Draw.

a

b

c

d

1

Your favourite season is winter!

Over To You

15 Play *Mime and guess!*

Key learning outcome: talk about the seasons
Language: *In (spring), you can see (flowers) on the tree. (My) favourite season is (winter).*

35

Lesson 7 Unit review

16 Listen, number and repeat. Complete the sentences.

2:17

a

I'm wearing a __coat__.

b

I'm wearing a _____.

c

I'm wearing a _____.

d

1

I'm wearing _____ and _____.

e

I'm wearing _____.

f

I'm _____ a _____.

g

I'm _____ a _____.

h

I'm _____ _____.

17 Look and write. Complete the sentence. ✏️

spring _____ _____ _____

_____ _____

My favourite season is _____.

18 Listen, point and repeat. Ask and answer. 🔊 2:18 💬

Is this your hat?

Class Chat

Learning to **LEARN**

➡️ Go to the Picture Dictionary on page 97.

1 Listen and say a traditional rhyme: *I'm a little snowman.*
Act it out. 2:19

I'm a little snowman.

2 Listen and number. Draw and write. 2:20

Comparing Cultures

a

scarf

b

T-shirt

c

jeans

In this picture, it's _____.
I'm wearing _____.

Key learning outcome: listen to, say and act out a traditional rhyme
Language: *I like (spring). It's my favourite season. In this picture, it's (winter). I'm wearing (a hat). jeans, scarf*

Break Time

Lesson 1 Vocabulary

1 Listen, look and repeat. 🔊 2:23 💬

2 Listen, point and say *Tiger's word chant*. 🔊 2:24 💬

3 Stick and say. Play *Can you remember?* 💬

1 board game

2 hide and seek

3 football

4 basketball

5 cards

6 tag

7 hopscotch

8 computer game

Key learning outcome: say and understand games vocabulary
Vocabulary: *board game, hide and seek, football, basketball, cards, tag, hopscotch, computer game*

Lesson 2 Story

4 Listen to the story. Answer the questions.
Play *Who says …?* 2:25

I want to play a computer game.

Do you want to play cards?

Has everyone got seven cards?

Li, have you got a four?

No, I haven't.

Sue, have you got a six?

Yes, I have.

Key learning outcome: listen to and understand a story
Story language: *I want to play (football). Do you want to play (cards)?*

5 I'm the winner.

I want to play again!

6 Tiger! You're cheating.

Sorry, everyone.

7 We don't want to play cards now.

I want to play basketball.

8 I'm sorry, Sue. Do you want to play a board game?

OK, but don't cheat.

Tiger Values

Do you play games fairly?

Lesson 3 Story activities

5 Listen and say the missing words. 🔊 💬
2:26

6 Listen and circle the game Tiger and the children play. 🔊 🎵 ✏️
2:27

Sing *I want to play*. Look and write.

1 board game

2

3

4

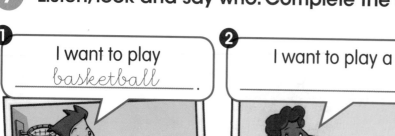

5

6

7

8

7 Listen, look and say who. Complete the sentences. 🔊 💬 ✏️
2:29

1 I want to play basketball .

2 I want to play a _____ .

3 I want to play _____ .

Jay

Anna

Tom

Key learning outcome: use games vocabulary and story language
Language: *I want to play (a computer game).*

Lesson 4 Speaking

8 Listen, look and say.
2:30

paint
games

Tiger Phonics

9 Make the cut-out on page 105. Do a role play.

> Do you want to play a board game?

> No, thanks. I want to play a computer game.

> Bingo!

Over To You

10 Play *Sentence bingo*.

Key learning outcome: practise pronunciation and do a role play
Language: *Do you want to play (a board game)? I want to play (a computer game).*
Phonics: *It's great to paint and play games at break time.*

School rules

Lesson 5 Cross-curricular

11 Listen, point and say. Read and stick. 2:31

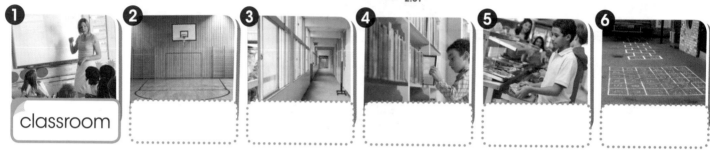

1. classroom
2.
3.
4.
5.
6.

12 Listen and repeat. Play *Observation*. 2:32

Ping and Pong

1. Can I play in the playground?

No, you can't. It's raining.

2.

3.

4. You can't play ball games in the classroom.

5.

6. Goal!

I want to play table football.

Key learning outcome: identify and talk about places in a school
Vocabulary: *classroom, gym, corridor, library, canteen, playground*

44

Lesson 6 Cross-curricular

13 Listen, number and repeat.
2:33

14 Listen and point. Sing *In the classroom*.
2:34
Cross (✗) where you can't play ball games.

a ✗

b 1

c

d

e

f

At my school, you can play cards in the classroom, but you can't play football.

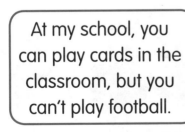
Over To You

15 Talk about your school.

Key learning outcome: talk about school rules
Language: *You can/can't (play ball games) in the (classroom).*

16 Listen, number and repeat. Complete the sentences.
2:35

a

I want to play ___basketball___.

b

I want to play ___hopscotch___.

c

I want to play a ___snakesandladders___

d

I want to play ___snap___.

e

I want to play a ___games___.

f

   1

I ___want to___ play ___Football___.

g

I ___want to___ play ___a hidandseek___.

h

I ___want to___ play ___tag___.

17 Look and write. Complete the sentences. ✏️

canteen

You can't play ball games in the _____.

You can play ball games in the _____

and the _____ .

18 Listen, point and repeat. Ask and answer. 🔊 💬
2:36

Do you want to sing a song?

Class Chat

➡️ Go to the Picture Dictionary on page 97.

Learning to LEARN

1 Listen and play the traditional game: *Rock, paper, scissors.* 🔊 2:37 💬 🎥

rock

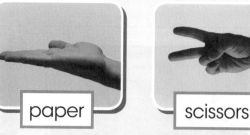

paper

scissors

2 Listen and number. Draw and write. 🔊 2:38 ✏️ ✏️

Comparing Cultures

computer game

leapfrog

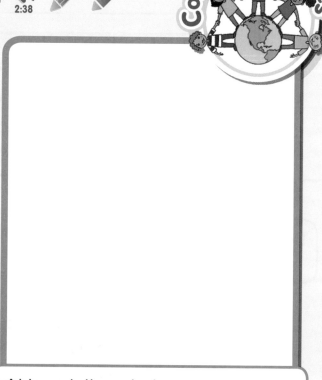

cards

At break time, I play _____
in the _____.

Key learning outcome: play a traditional game
Language: *At break time, I play (leapfrog) in the (playground). leapfrog, rock, paper, scissors*

Tiger Review 2

1 What games do you like to play?

2 Listen to the story. What games do Tiger and his friends play?
2:39

①

Do you want to play a board game?

Let's play 'Guess the season'.

② You're wearing a coat and a scarf ...

It's winter!

③

Let's play football.

④ This isn't a real football. It's a sockball!

⑤

Stop!

⑥ That's my favourite skirt!

Sorry. Time to tidy up?

3 What seasons are in the 'Guess the season' game?

4 Look, read and match. ✏️

1 **2** **3**

spring or autumn

summer

winter

5 Listen and circle. 🔊 ✏️
2:40

1			
2			
3			
4			

6 Listen and choose. 🔊
2:41
Sing your favourite song. 🎵

7 Think and colour. 💡 ✏️

Lesson 1 Vocabulary

1 Listen, look and repeat. 3:05

2 Listen, point and say *Tiger's word chant*. 3:06

3 Stick and say. Play *Can you remember?*

1 toothache   2 headache   3 cough   4 cut

5 earache   6 cold   7 tummy ache   8 sore throat

Key learning outcome: say and understand health vocabulary
Vocabulary: *toothache, headache, cough, cut, earache, cold, tummy ache, sore throat*

Lesson 2 Story

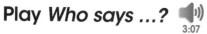

4 Listen to the story. Answer the questions.
Play *Who says ...?*
3:07

1

Hello, Jay. What's the matter?

I'm feeling ill. I've got a headache and a cold.

2

Hello, Doctor.

Hello. Come in.

3

I'm feeling ill. I've got earache.

What's the matter?

Please don't cry.

4

♪ *Don't be scared. Don't be sad.* 🎵

Key learning outcome: listen to and understand a story
Story language: *What's the matter? I'm feeling (ill). I've got (a headache).*

5 I'm feeling hot. I've got a sore throat and a cough.

6 ♪ *Doctors help us,* ♫ *So we don't feel bad.*

7 Thank you, Doctor.

8 Thank you, Tiger!

Tiger Values

How do you feel when you go to the doctor's?

Lesson 3 Story activities

5 Listen and say the missing words. 3:08

6 What's the matter with Sue and Jay? Listen and tick (✔).   3:09
Sing *I'm feeling ill.* Look and write.

1  ✔

cough

2

3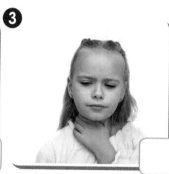

4

5

6

7

8

7 Listen, look and say who. Complete the sentences.   3:11

1 I'm feeling ill. I've got _earache_.

Sophie

2 I'm feeling ill. I've got a _____.

Tiger

3 I'm feeling ill. I've got _____.

Tom

Key learning outcome: use health vocabulary and story language
Language: *What's the matter? I'm feeling (ill). I've got (a headache).*

Lesson 4 Speaking

8 Listen, look and say.
3:12

Rob
hot

Tiger Phonics

9 Make the cut-out on page 107. Do a role play.

I'm feeling ill.

What's the matter?
Have you got a cut?

No, I haven't.

I've got a cold.

Over To You

10 Play *Have you got a cut?*

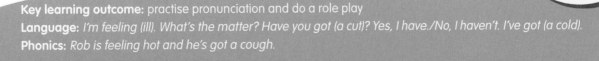
Key learning outcome: practise pronunciation and do a role play
Language: *I'm feeling (ill). What's the matter? Have you got (a cut)? Yes, I have./No, I haven't. I've got (a cold).*
Phonics: *Rob is feeling hot and he's got a cough.*

Keeping healthy

Lesson 5 Cross-curricular

11 Listen, point and say. Read and stick. 3:13

1 | drink water

2

3

4

5

6

12 Listen and repeat. Play *Observation*. 3:14

Ping and Pong

Key learning outcome: identify and talk about ways to keep healthy
Vocabulary: drink water, wash, do exercise, eat well, play, sleep well

Lesson 6 Cross-curricular

13 Listen, number and repeat.

3:15

14 Listen and point. Sing *Keep healthy*. Mime.

3:16

a

b

c

d

e

1

f

Do you sleep well every day?

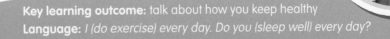

15 Play *Mime and ask.*

Key learning outcome: talk about how you keep healthy
Language: *I (do exercise) every day. Do you (sleep well) every day?*

Lesson 7 Unit review

16 **Listen, number and repeat. Complete the sentences.**
3:17

a SALLY

b MAX

c ALICE

d DAN

I've got a ___cold___ .

I've got a _____ .

I've _____ a _____ .

I've _____ _____ .

e JOE

f LEO 1

g LUCY

h LIZ

I've _____ a _____ .

I've _____ a _____ .

_____ _____ .

_____ _____ .

17 Look and write. Complete the sentences. ✏️

1

_____ sleep _____ well

2

_____ eat _____ well

3

_____ birycc exercise

4

_____ grihck water

5

_____ Play footbull

6

I _____ well every day.

I _____
every day.

18 Listen, point and repeat. Ask and answer. 🔊 3:18 💬

Class Chat

What's the matter?

➡️ Go to the Picture Dictionary on page 98.

Learning to **LEARN**

Kids' Culture

⑤

1 Listen and say the joke. Act it out. 🔊 3:19 💬 🎥

Doctor

Doctor, Doctor ...

2 Listen and number. Draw and write. 🔊 3:20 ✏️ ✏️

a
brush my teeth

b
eat well

c
do exercise

Comparing Cultures

I _____ every day.

Key learning outcome: listen to, say and act out a joke
Language: I (brush my teeth) every day.

6 On Holiday

Lesson 1 Vocabulary

1 Listen, look and repeat. 🔊 3:23 💬

2 Listen, point and say *Tiger's word chant*. 🔊 3:24 💬

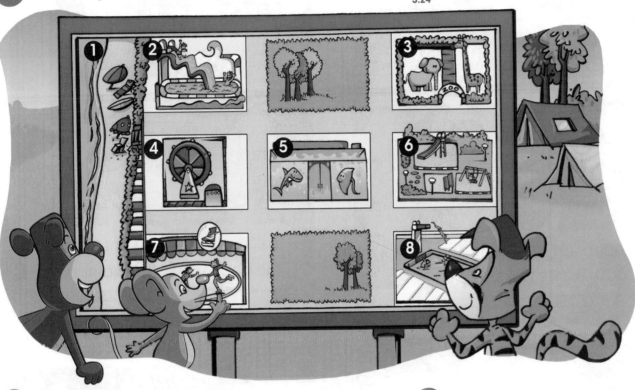

3 Stick and say. Play *Can you remember?* 💬

1 beach

2 water park

3 zoo

4 funfair

5 aquarium

6 park

7 ice rink

8 swimming pool

Key learning outcome: say and understand places vocabulary
Vocabulary: *beach, water park, zoo, funfair, aquarium, park, ice rink, swimming pool*

Lesson 2 Story

4 Listen to the story. Answer the questions.
Play *Who says ...?* 3:25

Key learning outcome: listen to and understand a story
Story language: *There's (an ice rink). Is there (an aquarium)? Yes, there is./No, there isn't.*

Tiger Values

When you make decisions, are you fair? Do you think about other people?

Lesson 3 Story activities

5 Listen and say the missing words.
3:26

6 Listen and tick (✔) the place the children go to.
3:27
Sing *In this town*. Look and write.

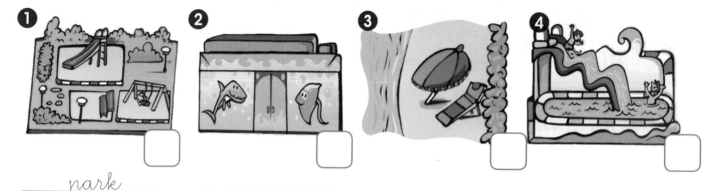

❶ ❷ ❸ ❹

park

❺ ❻ ❼ ❽

7 Listen, look and say who. Complete the sentences.
3:29

❶ In our town, there's a
park and a
zoo .

Sue

❷ In our town, there's a
_____ .

Jay

❸ In our town, there's
an _____ and
an _____ .

Li

Key learning outcome: use places vocabulary and story language
Language: *There's (a swimming pool).*

Lesson 4 Speaking

8 Listen, look and say.
3:30

hair
funfair

Tiger Phonics

9 Make the cut-out on page 109. Do a role play.

Is there a park?

Yes, there is.

There's a funfair.

Over To You

10 Play *In your town.*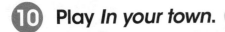

Key learning outcome: practise pronunciation and do a role play
Language: *Is there (a park)? Yes, there is./No, there isn't. There's (a funfair).*
Phonics: *There's a bear with pink hair at the funfair.*

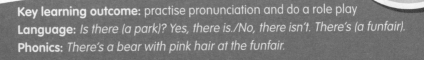

Road safety

Lesson 5 Cross-curricular

11 Listen, point and say. Read and stick.
3:31

1

stop

2

3

4

5

6

12 Listen and repeat. Play *Observation*.
3:32

Ping and Pong

1 Stop!

2

3

4 Look left and right, and listen.

5 You can cross the road now.

6

Key learning outcome: identify and talk about road safety rules
Vocabulary: *stop, stand on the pavement, look left, look right, listen, cross the road*

Lesson 6 Cross-curricular

13 Listen, number and repeat. 3:33

14 Listen and point. Sing *The road safety song*. 3:34
Talk about the signs and colour.

a

b

c

Look left and right.

Over To You

15 Say the road safety rules and mime.

Key learning outcome: talk about road safety rules and signs
Language: *Don't (stand in the road). stop, stand on the pavement,
look left, look right, listen, cross the road*

Lesson 7 Unit review

16 Listen, number and repeat. Complete the sentences.
3:35

a SALLY

Look! There's an ___aquarium___ .

b JOE   1

Look! There's a _____ .

c LIZ

Look! _____ a _____ .

d MAX

Look! _____ an _____ .

e ALICE

Look! _____ a _____ .

f DAN

Look! _____ .

g LUCY

Look! _____ .

h LEO

Look! _____ .

17 **Look and write. Complete the sentences.**

1

stop

2

on the pavement

3

_____ left

4

_____ right

5

_____

6

_____ the road

Look right and look _____, and _____ .

You can _____ _____ now.

18 **Listen, point and repeat. Ask and answer.**

3:36

Class Chat

Can I have a pencil, please?

➔ Go to the Picture Dictionary on page 98.

Learning to
LEARN

Kids' Culture

6

1 Listen and say a traditional rhyme: *A sailor goes to sea.* **Act it out.** 🔊 3:37 🎵 🎥

A sailor goes to sea, sea, sea …

2 Listen and number. Draw and write. 🔊 3:38 ✏️ ✏️

a park

b cinema

c swimming pool

Comparing Cultures

In my town, there's a _____ _____.

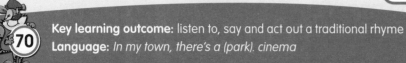
Key learning outcome: listen to, say and act out a traditional rhyme
Language: *In my town, there's a (park). cinema*

Tiger Review 3

Tiger and Friends

1 Where do you like to go in the holidays?

2 Listen to the story. What's the matter with Monkey? 🔊 📹 3:39

❶ It's holiday time, Tiger!

We can go to the swimming pool.

❷ I want to go to the beach.

❸ What's the matter, Monkey?

I've got a cut on my tail!

❹ Poor Monkey!

Where do you want to go, Monkey?

❺ Can we go to the aquarium?

Yes, of course.

❻ Wow! Are you real?

Yes. I'm real *and* I'm a toy.

3 Where does Monkey want to go?

4 Look and match.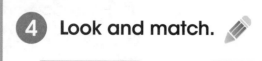

earache	cut	sore throat	tummy ache

1

2

3

4

5

6

7

8

headache	cold	toothache	cough

5 Listen and tick (✔) or cross (✗). 3:40

 ✔

6 Listen and choose. 3:41 Sing your favourite song.

7 Think and colour.

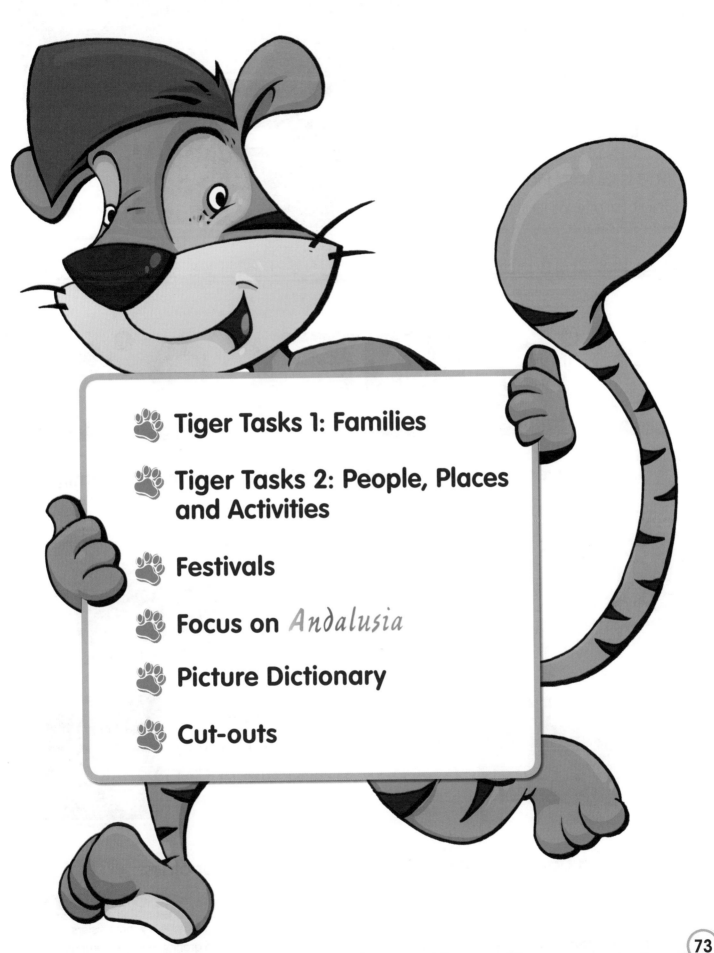

- 🐾 **Tiger Tasks 1: Families**

- 🐾 **Tiger Tasks 2: People, Places and Activities**

- 🐾 **Festivals**

- 🐾 **Focus on** *Andalusia*

- 🐾 **Picture Dictionary**

- 🐾 **Cut-outs**

1 Look and match.

This is Gerard Piqué and Shakira with their family. Who's in your family?

| **1** granny | **2** grandad | **3** mum | **4** dad | **5** sister | **6** brother |

 a
 b
 c
 d
 e
 f

2 Look and read. How many males and females are in each family?

Hi! I'm Victor. I've got a small family. I live with my mum and dad. I've got a grandad and two grannies.

5
4
3
2
1

Males   Females

5
4
3
2
1

Males   Females

Hello! My name's Maisie. I've got a mum, a dad and three sisters. I've got two grandads.

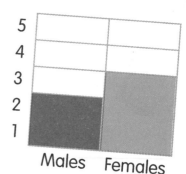

3 Make a bar graph of your family. Present it to your class.

Key learning outcome
Mathematics: read about and count family members using bar graphs

Language Help
a sister ⟶ three sisters
a granny ⟶ two grannies

A musical family

1 Look and match. Listen and check. 4:01

1 piano   **2** guitar   **3** sing   **4** dance

2 Look, listen and number. 4:02

1

3 Ask and answer.

What can you do?

I can sing and dance.
I can't play the piano.

Language Help

I **can** dance.
I **can't** play the piano.

Key learning outcome
Music: listen and identify different musical instruments

Helping at home

1 **Look and match. Listen and check.** 4:03

a wash the car **b** set the table **c** do the shopping

2 **Read Katy's letter and complete the sentences.**

> Dear David,
>
> This weekend, I've got to **do the shopping** with Dad.
> I've also got to **wash the dishes** with Mum and I've got
> to **set the table** with Grandad. I like helping at home!
> Do you help at home?
> Love from,
> Katy

1 Katy has got to help ___Dad___ do the shopping.

2 Katy has got to help _____ wash the dishes.

3 Katy has got to help _____ set the table.

3 **Look, read and complete David's letter.**

> Dear Katy,
> Yes, I help at home. This weekend, I've got to _____
> and I've got to _____. I like helping at home, too!
> Love from, David

Language Help

I've got to help Dad.
I've got to wash the dishes.

Key learning outcome
Social Science: write a letter about helping at home

Make a helping at home poster

Work in groups. Talk about how you can help at home and make a poster. Use the internet and language like this:

> We can help our parents do the shopping.

> I've got to clean my bedroom on Sunday.

> We've got to wash the dishes at dinnertime.

Step 1 Choose the tasks you can do at home.

do the shopping

wash the car

set the table

clean my bedroom

Step 2 Decide when to do the tasks.

We've got to wash the car on Saturday.
We've got to do the shopping on Friday.
We've got to wash the dishes at dinnertime.

Step 3 Make a poster to show how and when you can help.

Step 4 Present your poster to the class.

People, Places and Activities
On holiday

Reading

1 Look and match. Listen and check. 4:04

1 hike

2 fish

3 cycle

a the park

b the mountains

c the river

2 Read and say *True* or *False*.

Dear Uncle Bob,

This holiday is fantastic! It's very cold and snowy. Look at the **mountains**. You can **hike** in the mountains. It's really fun!

Love, Tina

Mr Bob Smith,
1 Cook Road,
London,
UK

✉ email 📎2

Hi Duncan,

How are you? I'm on holiday in **Scotland**. This is a photo of the beautiful **river**! You can **fish** in the river. There are lots of fish!

Do you like my photos?

From,
Tim

1 Tina is at the beach.

2 Tim is in Scotland.

3 Tim can fish in the river.

4 Tina can hike at the beach.

3 Draw a picture of a place and say.

In the park, you can play football and you can cycle.

Language Help

You can hike in the mountains.
You can cycle in the park.

Key learning outcome
Social Science: read and think about activities we can do outdoors

Daisy's calendar

1 **Look, listen and say the months.** 🔊 4:05 💬

January	February	March	April	May	June

July	August	September	October	November	December

2 **Write the missing dates on Daisy's calendar. Listen and check.** ✏️ 🔊 4:06

 This is my calendar for May. When is my birthday?

11th	30th	14th
26th	~~3rd~~	21st

May

Monday	Tuesday	Wednesday	Thursday	Friday	Saturday	Sunday
	1st	2nd My birthday! 🎁	a ___3rd___	4th	5th	6th
7th	8th	9th	10th	b _____	12th	13th
c _____	15th	16th	17th	18th Sports Day at school	19th	20th
d _____	22nd Dad's birthday	23rd	24th	25th	e _____	27th Go cycling with Rachel
28th	29th	f _____	31st			

3 **Look at Daisy's calendar again.**
Listen to the questions and answer. 🔊 4:07 💬

4 **Ask and answer.** 💬 👤

 When is your birthday?

My birthday is on the tenth of July.

Language Help

We write: 21st May
We say: the twenty-first of May

Key learning outcome
Mathematics: listen and understand a calendar

Holiday fact files

1 Read Ben's holiday fact file. What's his favourite holiday activity?

Ben's Holiday Fact File

Country: Spain

Place: Barcelona

Description: Barcelona is a big city. There are many **shops** and **tourists**. There are some great **parks**. There's a **beach**.

Favourite holiday activity: **playing football** on the beach

2 Read and complete Claire's holiday fact file. 🖊

There are lots of **mountains** in Cantabria, in **Spain**. My favourite place is the Picos de Europa. My favourite holiday activity is **hiking**. In the Picos de Europa, you can hike to **many different places.**

Claire's Holiday Fact File

Country: _____

Place: Picos de Europa, Cantabria

Description: There are lots of _____ .
You can hike to _____ different places.

Favourite holiday activity: _____

3 Write a holiday fact file for you. 🖊👤

Country: ...   Place: ...
Description: There are ... You can ...

Language Help
There are **some** parks.
There are **lots of** mountains. There are **many** shops.

Key learning outcome
Social Science: write a fact file and learn about two places

Make a collage of a place

Work in groups or pairs. Make a collage to represent a place that you all like. Use the internet and language like this:

> There are lots of tall buildings.

> There are some swings.

> You can swim in the sea.

Step 1 Choose a place that you like.

the park

the mountains

the city

the beach

Step 2 Think of three things you can do at the place.

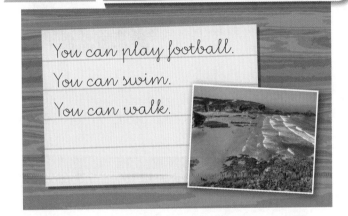

You can play football.
You can swim.
You can walk.

Step 3 Find pictures of your place and make a collage.

The beach

Step 4 Write about your place and present your collage to the class.

The beach
There are some big rocks.
You can swim.
You can walk.
You can play football.

HALLOWEEN

1 Listen and point. Mime and say. 4:08

1 monster

2 spider

3 wizard

4 moon

5 skeleton

2 Listen and find. Sing *Halloween night.* 4:09

Key learning outcome: say and understand Halloween vocabulary
Vocabulary: *monster, spider, wizard, moon, skeleton*

3 Listen and look. Say *True* or *False*.

4:10

4 Listen, match and repeat. 4:11

① 　② 　③ 　④

ⓐ 　ⓑ 　ⓒ 　ⓓ

5 Make the Halloween box (TB, p172). Do a role play.

Over To You

I've got a surprise for you.

Key learning outcome: make a Halloween box and do a role play
Language: *I've got a surprise for you. What is it? Look in the box. It's a (monster). Happy Halloween!*

Christmas

1 Listen and point. Mime and say.
4:12

1 Father Christmas

2 Christmas card

3 Christmas stocking

4 Christmas cake

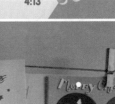

5 snowflake

2 Listen and find. Sing *Christmas cards everywhere.*
4:13

Key learning outcome: say and understand Christmas vocabulary
Vocabulary: *Father Christmas, Christmas card, Christmas stocking, Christmas cake, snowflake*

3 Look and write. Find and circle. ✏️

1
F a t h e r
Christmas

2
Christmas
_ _ _ _ _

3
Christmas
_ _ _ _ _ _ _

S	N	O	W	F	L	A	K	E
T	A	K	Q	Z	V	B	D	P
O	D	C	C	S	D	R	Q	H
C	Y	F	A	T	H	E	R	P
K	I	L	K	B	J	Y	U	M
I	L	Y	E	A	G	J	H	C
N	M	E	B	U	Y	R	W	S
G	V	W	N	J	C	A	R	D

4
_ _ _ _ _ _ _ _

5
Christmas
_ _ _ _

4 Listen, match and repeat. 🔊 4:14 ✏️ 💬

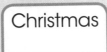

1  **2**  **3**  **4**

a  **b**  **c**  **d**

5 Make the Christmas card (TB, p173). Do a role play. ✂️ 💬

Over To You

Look! I've got a Christmas card.

Key learning outcome: make a Christmas card and do a role play
Language: *Look! I've got a Christmas card. What's the picture? It's (Father Christmas). Happy Christmas!*

Carnival

1 Listen and point. Mime and say.
4:15

1
king

2
pirate

3
cowboy

4
queen

5
clown

2 Listen and find. Sing *It's Carnival time*.
4:16

Key learning outcome: say and understand Carnival vocabulary
Vocabulary: *king, pirate, cowboy, queen, clown*

3 Listen and say. Colour the hats. 🔊 4:17 💬 ✏️

4 Listen, match and repeat. 🔊 4:18 ✏️ 💬

5 Make the Carnival mask (TB, p174).
Do a role play. ✂️ 💬

I'm wearing fancy dress. What am I?

Key learning outcome: make a Carnival mask and do a role play
Language: It's Carnival time. I'm wearing fancy dress. What am I? You're a (pirate).

87

Topic 1 **Places in Andalusia**

Vocabulary

Hi, I'm Lucía. I live in Grazalema. My favourite place is the forest. Where's your favourite place?

1 **Look and circle.**

1 (beach) / shop   2 castle / forest   3 mountain / cave   4 river / square

5 forest / cave   6 shop / mountain   7 river / castle   8 square / beach

2 **Look. Read and write *Yes* or *No*.**

1 The beach is **between** the river and the mountain. No
2 The mountain is **behind** the forest. _____
3 The cave is **near** the beach. _____
4 The forest is **next to** the river. _____
5 The river is **in front of** the cave. _____

3 **Read and match.**

1 You can go skiing here.   beach
2 You can buy food and clothes here.   mountain
3 You can go swimming here.   shop

Read a postcard

1 **Read and number.**

Dear Granny and Grandad,
I'm in El Bosque with Mum and Dad. It is very beautiful and the weather is sunny and very hot.

[ ] There's a river called the Majaceite. The river is in a beautiful forest, and you can walk through the forest to the next village.

[1] There's a botanical garden and there are lots of different trees.

[ ] There are lots of good restaurants and you can eat delicious fish.

See you soon!
Love,
María

ESPAÑA 50

2 **Read and circle.**

1 You can walk **next to** / **through** the forest to the next village.
2 There are **some** / **lots of** different trees in the botanical garden.
3 There's a **river** / **square** called the Majaceite.
4 In the restaurants you can eat delicious **meat** / **fish**.

3 **Talk to your friend about El Bosque.**

Is there a beach in El Bosque?

No, there isn't.

Are there restaurants in El Bosque?

Yes, there are.

Read and write a text message

1 **Read and write.**

Hi, Isabel! How are you? I'm fine. I'm in Aracena. There are some fantastic caves and there's a castle. Bye, David.

Hi, Alicia! How are you? I'm well. I'm in Málaga. There are some great shops and there's a beautiful square. Bye, Daniel.

1 Who is the text message to?
Isabel

2 Who is the text message from?
David

3 Where is he?
Aracena

4 What can you see there?
Caves and a castle

1 Who is the text message to?
_____

2 Who is the text message from?
_____

3 Where is he?
_____

4 What can you see there?
_____

2 **Do you write text messages?**

3 **Plan your text message.**

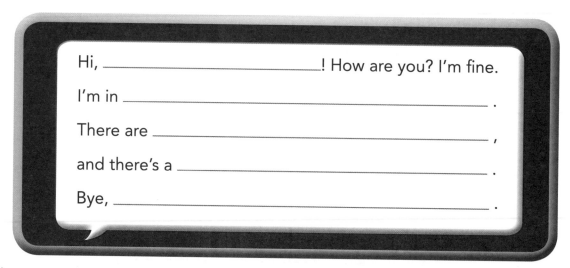

Hi, _____! How are you? I'm fine.

I'm in _____ .

There are _____ ,

and there's a _____ .

Bye, _____ .

4 **Draw a mobile phone and copy your message.**

Final task: Do a project

Create a postcard.
Investigate and use the internet. Use this language:

> Let's ...

> Good idea!

> We can ...

Step 1	Choose a place.

Step 2	Find or draw pictures.

Step 3	Write your message.

We're in Nerja.

There's an aqueduct and there are big caves.

You can listen to music in the caves.

Step 4	Present your postcard.

We're in Nerja.
There's an aqueduct and there are big caves.
You can listen to music in the caves.

Topic 2 — Food in Andalusia

Vocabulary

Hi, I'm Rafa. I live in Cazalla de la Sierra. My favourite food is lentils. What's your favourite food?

1 Look and number.

a	fried fish	
b	meatballs	
c	shrimp fritters	1
d	Spanish omelette	
e	egg and chips	
f	cold tomato soup	
g	lentils	
h	spinach and chickpeas	

2 Find and circle.

Spanish **omelette**   shrimp **fritters**

fried fish   **meatballs**

egg and **chips**   **spinach** and chickpeas

cold tomato **soup**   **lentils**

O	S	C	S	G	R	S	O	U	P
M	E	A	T	B	A	L	L	S	M
E	S	L	E	F	U	Y	C	O	C
L	P	D	W	X	N	P	H	H	J
E	I	M	L	E	N	T	I	L	S
T	N	N	S	R	J	P	P	L	M
T	A	N	D	S	S	L	S	W	V
E	C	H	B	X	F	R	I	E	D
T	H	F	R	I	T	T	E	R	S

3  What food do you eat where you live? Draw and write.

_____

Read a tourism webpage

1 **Read and number.**

ANDALUSIAN FESTIVALS

The Feria in Seville is usually in April. You can see lots of horses and beautiful dresses. People eat fried fish and Spanish omelette and they dance very well!

In Córdoba, people celebrate the Patios. In May, you can see patios with lots of beautiful flowers and you can eat Córdoba's famous cold tomato soup.

Cádiz has a big carnival in February. You can see lots of fantastic costumes and you can eat the delicious shrimp fritters. 2

2 **Read and write.**

	Feria in Seville	The Patios in Córdoba	Carnival in Cádiz
When is the festival?	April		
What can you see?	horses, beautiful dresses		
What can you eat?	fried fish, Spanish omelette		

3 **Talk to your friend about the festivals.**

When is the Feria in Seville?

In April.

What can you see?

You can see horses and beautiful dresses.

What can you eat?

You can eat fried fish and Spanish omelette.

Read and write a birthday party invitation

> ### Come to my Birthday Party!
>
> **To:** Daniel
>
> **Where?** Jerez de la Frontera
>
> **When?** 4th May
>
> **What are we going to do?** see the dancing horses
>
> **What are we going to eat?** egg and chips, ice cream, birthday cake
>
> **From:** Alejandro

1 **Read and circle.**

1 The invitation is to **Daniel** / **Alejandro**.

2 The party is in **Córdoba** / **Jerez de la Frontera**.

3 The party is on **4th May** / **4th April**.

4 They are going to see **birds** / **horses**.

5 They are going to eat **Spanish omelette** / **egg and chips**.

2 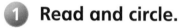 **When is your birthday?**

3 **Plan your birthday party invitation.**

> ### Come to my birthday party!
>
> To: _____
>
> Where? _____
>
> When? _____
>
> What are we going to do? _____
>
> What are we going to eat? _____
>
> From: _____

4 **Copy and decorate your invitation.**

Final task: Do a project

Create and present a restaurant menu.
Investigate and use the internet. Use this language:

How about ...?

We can have ...

I like ...

Step 1 Choose a name for your restaurant.

The Old Restaurant

MANOLO'S CAFÉ

THE FISH HOUSE

Step 2 Choose four dishes.

Step 3 Think of your prices.

€5

€3.50

€1

€2.50

Step 4 Present your menu.

THE FISH HOUSE

Fried fish	€5
Shrimp fritters	€2.50
Spanish omelette	€1
Spinach and chickpeas	€3.50

Picture Dictionary

Unit 1

bathroom

Unit 2

bird

Unit 3

coat

Unit 4

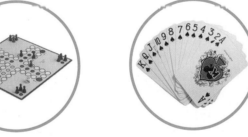

basketball

Unit 5

cold

_____ _____ _____ _____

_____ _____ _____ _____

Unit 6

aquarium

_____ _____ _____ _____

_____ _____ _____ _____

Lesson 4 Make the cut-out. Do a role play.

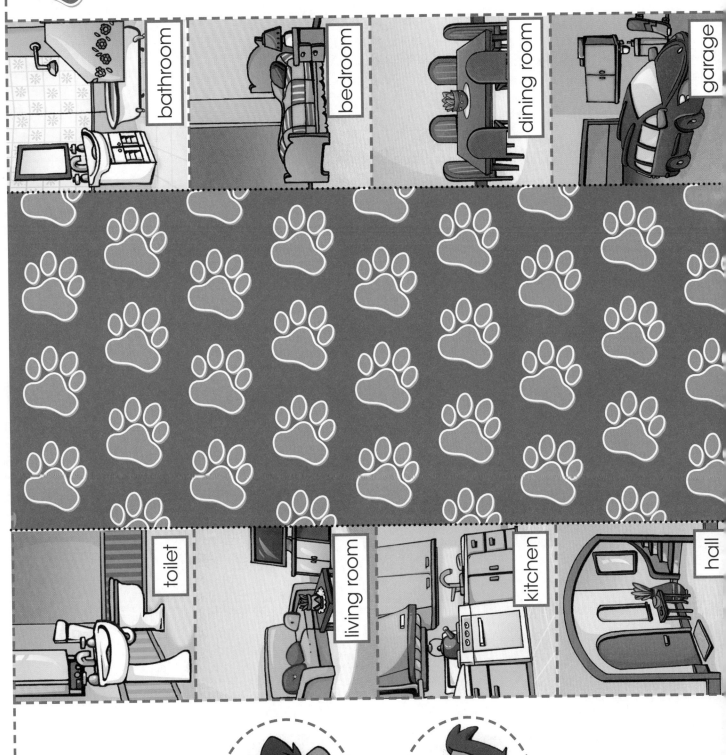

bathroom

bedroom

dining room

garage

toilet

living room

kitchen

hall

Lesson 4   Make the cut-out. Do a role play.

bird

fish

rabbit

turtle

hamster

puppy

kitten

lizard

hat

jumper

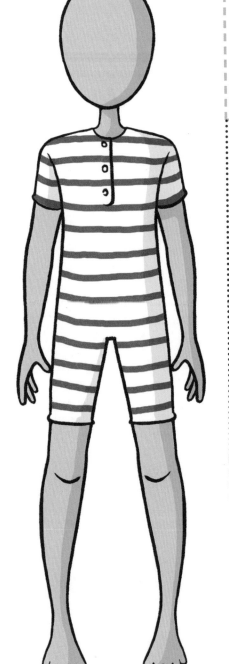

T-shirt

shorts

trousers

shoes

socks

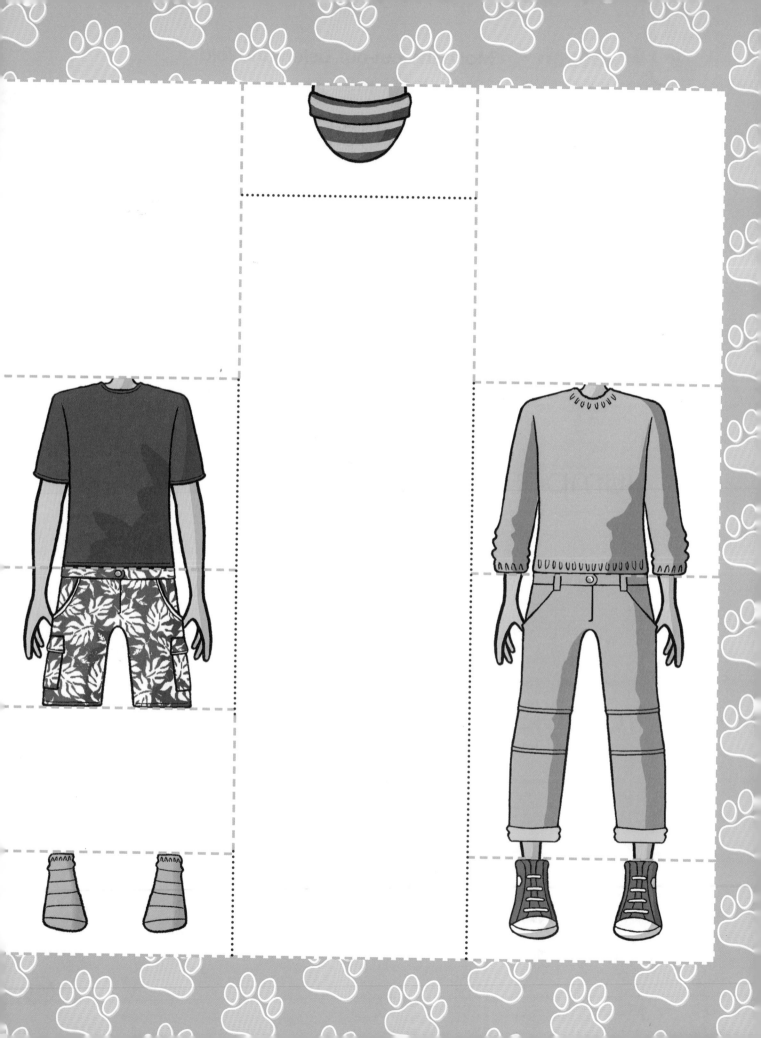

Lesson 4 Make the cards. Do a role play.

a sore throat

a cold

a headache

a cut

a cough

tummy ache

earache

toothache

Lesson 4 Make the cut-out. Do o___ __ay.

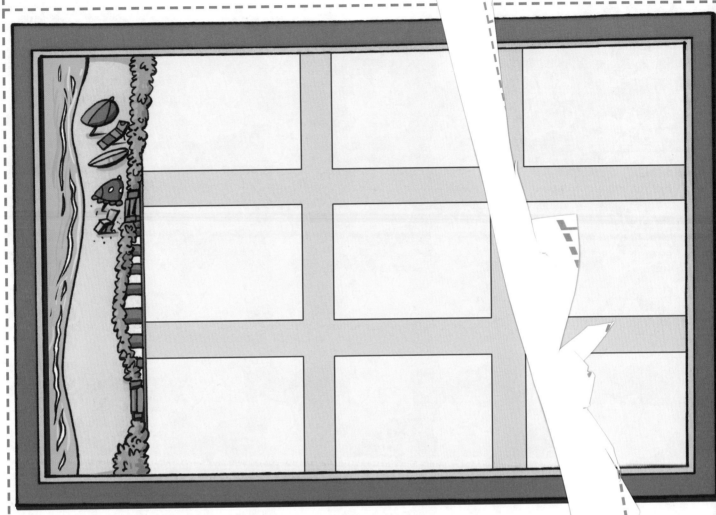

Macmillan Education
4 Crinan Street
London N1 9XW
A division of Springer Nature Limited

Companies and representatives throughout the world

New Tiger Level 2 Pupil's Book Andalusian Edition ISBN 978-1-380-04560-7
New Tiger Level 2 Pupil's Book Pack Andalusian Edition ISBN 978-1-380-03754-1

Original design by Blooberry Design Ltd
This edition design and page make-up by emc design ltd
Illustrated by Philip Hailstone, Ricard Zaplana Ruiz and Eric Smith
(all Beehive Illustration); Rodrigo Folgueira (Illustopia), Tony Forbes, Kelly Kennedy and Jo Taylor (all Sylvie Poggio); Jan McCafferty and Anthony Rule.
Cover design by Astwood Design Consultancy and Designers Collective
Cover illustration by Anthony Rule
Cover images provided by **Getty Images**/Marques Photography; **Springer Nature Limited**/Getty/iStockphoto/tifonimages, STOCKBYTE.
Author photograph (Carol Read) by Michael Selley
Picture research by Victoria Gaunt and Julie-anne Wilce

Additional material for Andalusia
Designed by Nicola Paull (Bigmouse Design)
Illustrated by Simon Walmesley
Picture research by Haremi Ltd.

Authors' acknowledgements
We would like to thank everyone at Macmillan Education in the UK and in Spain who has helped us in the development and the production of these materials. We would also like to thank all the teachers who have taken time to read, pilot and give feedback at every stage of writing the course. Special thanks from Carol to Alan, Jamie and Hannah for their encouragement and support. Special thanks from Mark to Carlos for his patience and understanding.

The authors and publishers would like to thank the following for permission to reproduce their photographs:
Alamy a-plus image bank p92(5), age forostock p90(r), Art of Food pp92,95(3),(l), Ian Allenden p74(br), Arcaid Images pp7(1), 12(1), 96(cr), Stuart Black p89(c), Sergey Borisov p91(l), BSIP SA p98(tcl), Nicholas Burningham p92(r), Mike Cumberbatch p88(l), Ros Drinkwater p90(l), Sergey Dzyuba p91(r), Emilio Ereza pp92.95(8),(r), eurekaimages.com p97(mcl), Jesus Noguera Fernandez p92(l), Peter Forsberg p89(r), Image Source p86(4), Ruslan Kudrin pp29(2), 97(tcr), Tony Lilley p98(cr), Jose Manuel Revuelta Luna p93(l), Maxstock p97(mcr), Steven May p59(3), MBI pp44(1), 47(2), 70(a), juan moyano p92(6), Panther Media GmbH p91(c), New photos by Alfonso de Tomas p92(1), Myrleen Pearson p19(br), Picturamic pp44(6), 47(6), Chico Sanchez p89(l), Sandra van der Steen p82(2), Maria Galan Still p92(2), RayArt Graphics p84(b), Ket Sang Tai p92(4), Lucas Vallecillos p93(r), Rob Walls p63(bc); **Fotolia** Pressmaster pp16(t,t,t), 26(t,t,t), 38(t,t,t), 48(t,t,t), 60(t,t,t), 70(t,t,t); **Getty Images** Adventtr pp7(2), 96(tcl), 97(tr), alex_kz p81(glue), altrendo images p67(a), Anadolu Agency p74(t), aoldman p81(park), Art Vandalay p38(a), Asia selects p38(b), Asiseeit p44(5), Mark Edward Atkinson p15(bl), Eric Audras p74(b), Baona p57(5), Alistair Berg p57(3), Bgfoto pp22(5), 25(4), Walter Bibikow p98(bcl), Blend Images/JGI p57(2), Blend Images/KidStock p76(3), 77(set), Bowden images p60(b), J Bryson p54(7), Chris Close p34(6), 37(6), Steve Cole pp6(cr), 15(cr), 25(cr), 37(cr), 47(cr), 59(cr), 69(cr), Compassionate Eye Foundation/Martin Barraud p25(bl), Andy Crawford p82(1), Håkan Dahlström p97(bcr), Daly and Newton p86(br), Catherine Delahaye p26(a), Dorling Kindersley p84(2), Echo p81(family)(bc), eli_asenova p80(tl), EschCollection p98(bl), FatCamera p9(bc), filipefrazao p81(city), Floresco Productions p48(a), Fuse p47(br), 84(5), Glow Décor p12(4), Glow Wellness p55(bl), Rick Gomez pp53(bc), 74(a), Steve Gorton pp29(4), 97(tcl), Manfred Gottschalk p81(beach)(cr), Jeff Greenough p41(br), Jamie Grill pp8(tr), 18(tr), 30(tr), 33(bl), 40(tr), 52(tr), 62(tr), 75(c), Tom Grill p56(6), Tim Hall p48(b), Hero Images p15(bc), Michael Hewes p82(b), Highwaystarz-Photography p47(bl), Hybrid Images pp76(1), 77(shop), Image Source pp54(4), 75(b), 98(tcr), Image Studio p70(b), Inti St Clair p75(a), JackF p78(cr), jamesdvdsn p82(bl), jaroon p79(bl), Johner Images p81(swim,br), Huw Jones p84(4), Jose Luis Pelaez Inc p74(e,cl), Milan_Jovic p67(c), Juice Images Ltd pp57(1), 81(football,b), Julian Elliott Photography p78(c), Jupiterimages p59(bc), JurgaR p86(5), ka2shka p54(3), Kdshutterman p51(1), Mike Kemp pp76(2), 77(wash), KidStock pp74(f), 86(2), Dave King pp29(3), 97(tl), Kroeger/Gross p12(2), Rob Lewine p45(bl), LOOK-foto/Bernard van Dierendonck p78(c), Tim Macpherson p74(c), MarquesPhotography p80(br), MILATAS pp44(3), 47(3),

Monkeybusinessimages pp19(bc), 80(tl), mustafagull p98(cmr), Margus Muts p82(4), Niedring/Drentwett p45(e), Nycshooter p59(br), Gary Ombler p82(3), Lori Adamski Peek p26(c), People Images p77(tidy), alan phillips p78(a), Ray Pietro p16(a), Tim Platt p59(4), Steve Prezant p16(b), Susanna Price p86(br), Purestock p98(br), Stephanie Rausser p9(br), REB Images p74(d), Andersen Ross p15(br), RPM Pictures p45(cl), Science Photo Library p98(cr), Shih-Hao Liao p97(mcr), Sizun Eye p78(river), SolStock p45(c,d), TEK IMAGE p53(br), T.T. p25(bc), Tuan Tran pp66(1), 69(1), utah778 p98(tr), Klaus Vedfelt p45(a), Victor p78(1,2,3), Vitapix p54(2), Wavebreakmedia Ltd pp26(b), 45(f), 54(5), 66(5), 69(5), Ben Welsh pp66(3,4), 69(3,4), Westend61 pp78(b), 81(mountain), Julien de Wilde pp66(2,6), 69(2,6), Christoph Wilhelm pp44(2), 47(4), Mitch York p67(b); **Glow Images** Jose Luis Pelaez Inc p86(1); **Science Photo Library** JURGEN MAGG p41(bc); **Shutterstock** Africa Studio p54(8), Evgeniya Anikienko p38(c), Hung Chung Chih p59(1), Design Pics Inc p97(tr), Dream_Stock pp75(br), 77(tr), Freedom Studio p54(1), from my point of view p92(7), Littlekidmoment p78(b), mubus7 p98(cmr), MZinchenko p75(bl), PAKULA PIOTR p44(4), 47(5), pzRomashka p54(6), Rene Ramos p35(a,b,c,d), Rex/Image Source p98(cr), sanneberg p79(cl), SLP_London p75(d), SpeedKingz p45(b), 47(1), Syda Productions p97(br), Gladskikh Tatiana p56(1), Valua Vitaly p80(cr), Wavebreakmedia p47(bc), West Coast Surfer/Mood Board p82(5); **Springer Nature Limited** p22(3,4), 25(2,3), BANANASTOCK pp39(2), 60(a), 63(br), 97(cml), 98(cl), BRAND X pp7(6), 34(4), 37(4), 84(1,3), 96(tct,tr), Paul Bricknell pp39(1), 56(2), 59(6), 79(br), 81(scissors), 96(mcl), 97(cml), 88(r), Corbis pp39(4), 97(cl), 98(tl), Haddon Davies pp29(1), 97(cl), Getty Images p22(1,2,6), 23(1), 25(1,5,6), 34(5), 37(5), 39(3), 70(c), 97(bl), Getty/Blend Images/Marc Romanelli p59(bl), Getty/monkeybusinessimage p60(c), Getty/iStock/Thinkstock/Ivana Dukcevic Budja pp34(2), 37(2), Getty/iStock/Thinkstock/Michel de Nijs p56(3), Getty/iStock/Thinkstock/Szepy p81(tr), Getty/Brian E. Kushner p82(bl), ImageSource pp12(5), 98(cml), IStock pp56(5), 59(5), JOHN FOXX IMAGES pp17(3), 23(4), 96(mcl), JUPITER pp56(4), 59(2), Pa p57(4), PHOTODISC pp7(4,5), 12(6), 17(5,2,6,4), 21(cl), 23(1,5,3), 34(1,3), 37(1,3), 96(cl,mcr,bcr,mcr,bcl,bl,cr), PIXTAL p48(rock, paper, scissors), STOCKBYTE p12(3), David Tolley p97(cr), www.imagesource.com p61(1); **Superstock** Blend Images p86(3), Bost Anne-Sophie/Oredia Eurl p57(6), EWA Stock pp7(3), 96(tl), Glow Images p25(br), Juniors pp17(1), 96(cl), Kablonk p98(bcr), Science Photo Library p98(cml), Chevalier Virginie/Oredia Eurl p48(c).

Stickers
Alamy BSIP SA, eurekaimages.com, Shih-Hao Liao, Tony Lilley, maxstock; **Getty Images** adventtr, Walter Bibikow, Håkan Dahlström, EschCollection, Steve Gorton, Image Source, Dave King, Purestock, Science Photo Library, utah778; **Shutterstock** REX/Design Pics Inc, REX/Image Source, Syda Productions; **Springer Nature Limited** BANANASTOCK, Brand x, Paul Bricknell, Corbis, Haddon Davies, Getty, JOHN FOXX IMAGES, PHOTODISC; **Superstock** EWA Stock, Kablonk, Science Photo Library.

Commissioned photography by Stuart Cox pp6(a,b,c,d), 11(c,bl), 13(bl), 16(tl,c), 21(c,bl), 23(bl), 26(tl), 31(bc,br), 33(c), 35(bl), 37(bl,bc,br), 38(cl), 43(c,bl), 48(tl), 55(c), 57(bl), 60(tl), 65(c,bl), 67(bl), 69(bl,br), 70, (tl)83(bl), 85(bl), 87(bl).
Thanks to Mica, Christiana and Harry.

Printed and bound in Spain
2023 2022 2021 2020 2019
10 9 8 7 6 5 4 3 2 1

Unit 1

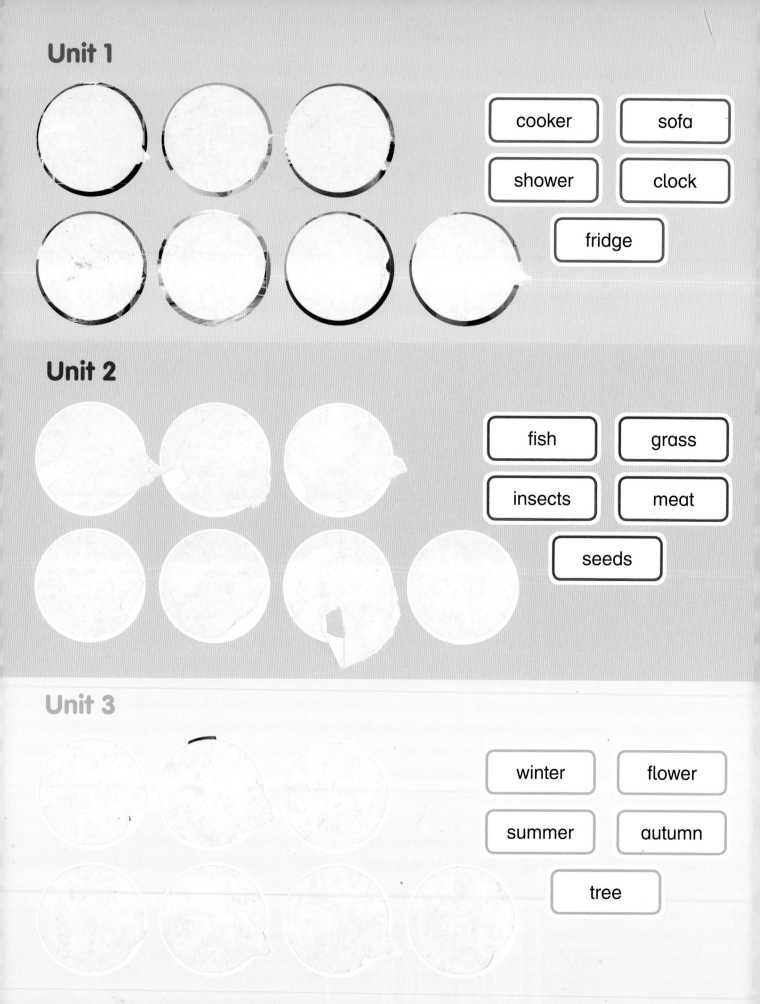

cooker
sofa
shower
clock
fridge

Unit 2

fish
grass
insects
meat
seeds

Unit 3

winter
flower
summer
autumn
tree

Unit 4

canteen   corridor

playground   library

gym

Unit 5

do exercise   sleep well

play   eat well

wash

Unit 6

look right   cross the road

listen   stand on the pavement

look left

mom

7
0
20
111

1277

b 7 12 1 8 100000 5004 12 Henrg

1881000